AMERICA IN THE TIME OF
FRANKLIN DELANO ROOSEVELT

1929 to 1948

Sally Senzell Isaacs

Published by Heinemann Library,
an imprint of Reed Educational & Professional Publishing,
100 N. LaSalle, Suite 1010 Chicago, IL 60602
Customer Service 888-454-2279
Visit our website at www.heinemannlibrary.com

AMERICA IN THE TIME OF FRANKLIN DELANO ROOSEVELT
was produced for Heinemann Library
by Bender Richardson White.

Editor: Lionel Bender
Designer: Ben White
Assistant Editor: Michael March
Picture Researcher: Pembroke Herbert
Media Conversion and Typesetting: MW Graphics
Production Controller: Kim Richardson

04 03 02 01 00
10 9 8 7 6 5 4 3 2

Printed in Hong Kong

Library of Congress Cataloging-in-Publication Data.
Isaacs, Sally, 1950–
    America in the time of Franklin Delano Roosevelt : the story of our
    nation from coast to coast, from 1929–1948 / Sally Senzell Isaacs.
        p.   cm.
Includes bibliographical references and index.
Summary: Uses the life of Franklin D. Roosevelt as a reference to
    examine the history of the United States from 1929 to 1948.
ISBN 1-57572-761-7 (lib. bdg.) 1-57572-938-5 (pbk.)
[1. United States–History–1933-1945–Juvenile literature.
    2. United States–History–1919-1933–Juvenile literature. 3. United
    States–History–1945-1953–Juvenile literature. 4. Roosevelt, Franklin D.
    (Franklin Delano), 1882-1945–Juvenile literature.] I. Title.
E806.I75   1999
973.917'092-dc21
                                                        99–20966
                                                        CIP

Special thanks to Mike Carpenter, Scott Westerfield, and Tristan Boyer at
Heinemann Library for editorial and design guidance and direction.

Photo Credits:
Picture Research Consultants, Mass: pages 11t (Franklin D. Roosevelt
Library, Hyde Park, New York), 11b (University of Washington Library,
Seattle, Washington), 12 (Franklin D. Roosevelt Library, Hyde Park, New
York/ACME), 13 (Franklin D. Roosevelt Library, Hyde Park, New York), 16
(PhotoAssist, Inc./National Archives), 17, 20b (Franklin D. Roosevelt
Library, Hyde Park, New York/World Wide), 22, 26 (National Archives), 28
(Franklin D. Roosevelt Library, Hyde Park, New York), 30, 32 (U.S. Army
Photograph/National Archives), 35c (Robert F. Sargent/Library of
Congress), 36 (National Archives: Suitland, courtesy of the United States
Holocaust Memorial Museum), 37 (National Archives). Peter Newark's
American Pictures: pages 7t, 7b, 8, 9, 15t, 15b, 18, 19, 20t, 23, 27, 31,
40, 41. Peter Newark's Military Pictures: 29, 33, 35t, 35b, 39t, 39b.
AKG Photo London: 25 (E. Gnilka).

Every effort has been made to contact copyright holders of any material
reproduced in this book. Omissions will be rectified in subsequent printings
if notice is given to the publisher.

Artwork credits
Illustrations by: John James on pages 6/7, 12/13, 14/15, 16/17, 24/25,
26/27, 28/29, 32/33, 36/37 ; Gerald Wood on pages 8/9, 10/11,
22/23, 30/31, 38/39; James Field on pages 18/19, 34/35, 40/41.
All maps by Stefan Chabluk.
Cover: Design and make-up by Pelican Graphics. Artwork by John James.
Photos: all from Peter Newark's American or Military Pictures.

Major quotations used in this book come from the
following sources. Some of the quotations have been
abridged for clarity.
Page 14: Letter from Dust Bowl from *Down and Out in the
Great Depression*, edited by Robert S. McElvaine. Chapel
Hill: University of North Carolina Press,1983, page 75.
Page 16: Roosevelt speech in Atlanta on November 29,
1935, from *Public Papers and Addresses of Franklin D.
Roosevelt (1935)*, edited by Samuel I. Rosenman. New
York: Harper & Bros., 1950, page 474.
Pages 24: Roosevelt State of the Union speech, January
6, 1941.
Page 26: Churchill's conversation with F.D.R. from *The
Second World War* by Winston Churchill and the Editors of
Life. New York: Golden Press, 1960, page 153.
Page 26: Roosevelt's address to Congress on December
8, 1941.
Page 27: F.D.R. speaking to Grace Tully from Tully's
account in *Eyewitness to America*, edited by David
Colbert. New York: Pantheon Books, 1997, page 405.
Page 34: Andy Rooney's quote from *My War* by Andy
Rooney. New York: Times Books/Random House, Inc.,
1995, page 151.
Page 38: F.D.R.'s proposed speech from *Roosevelt: The
Soldier of Freedom* by James MacGregor Burns. New
York: Smithmark Publishers, Inc., 1970, page 597.

The Consultants
Special thanks go to Diane Smolinski and
Nancy Cope for their help in the preparation of
this series. Diane Smolinski has years of
experience interpreting standards documents
and putting them into practice in fourth and
fifth grade classrooms. Nancy Cope splits her
time between teaching high school history,
chairing her department, training new teachers
at North Carolina State University, and being
President of the North Carolina Council for
Social Studies.

The Author
Sally Senzell Isaacs is a professional writer and
editor of nonfiction books for children. She
graduated from Indiana University, earning a
B.S. degree in Education with majors in
American History and Sociology. For some
years, she was the Editorial Director of
Reader's Digest Educational Division. Sally
Senzell Isaacs lives in New Jersey with her
husband and two children.

CONTENTS

America in the Time of is a series of nine books arranged chronologically, meaning that events are described in the order in which they happened. However, since each book focuses on an important person in American history, the timespans of the titles overlap. In each book, most articles deal with a particular event or part of American history. Others deal with aspects of everyday life, such as trade, houses, clothing, and farming. These general articles cover longer periods of time. The little illustration at the top left of each article is a symbol of the times. They are identified on page 3.

▼ **About the map**

This map shows the United States today. It shows the boundaries and names of all the states. Refer to this map, or to the one on pages 42–43, to locate places talked about in this book.

About this book

This book is about America from 1929 to 1948. The term America means "the United States of America" (also called the U.S.). The United States suffered severe economic depressions five times in its history. This book covers the worst depression in our history: the Great Depression that began in 1929. World War II (WWII) was a long, complicated struggle between many nations of the world. This book focuses on America's role in the war and how it affected the lives of U.S. citizens. Words in **bold** are described in more detail in the Glossary on page 46.

INTRODUCTION

The years between 1929 and 1948 were very good and very bad. The 1920s had been a happy and prosperous time for the country. Cars, radios, and motion pictures helped Americans enjoy more experiences. Factories made more goods than ever before, and jobs were more plentiful. By the end of 1929, the country had plunged into the worst economic conditions in history. The economic crisis affected not only the United States, but also Britain and many other European industrialized nations. All across America, millions of citizens lost their jobs, homes, and farms. These people worried that they could not feed their families. With high unemployment, some Americans turned to crime to make a living.

In 1932, Franklin Delano Roosevelt—his name was usually shortened to just F.D.R.—stepped into the job of United States president. He promised to give Americans jobs, food, and most of all, hope for the future. He worked hard to keep this promise as America struggled through the 1930s. By early 1942, factories were running and people were working again, mainly because America was getting involved in World War II. Americans, at home and abroad, helped win the war. As the 1940s came to a close, Americans once again enjoyed peace and prosperity.

Most of the events in this book took place during Roosevelt's life. On pages that describe events that happened in his lifetime but were not directly connected to him, there are yellow boxes that tell you what he and his family were doing at the time.

THE LAST OF THE GOOD TIMES

Franklin D. Roosevelt
F.D.R. was born on January 30, 1882. He grew up in a large, fancy house in Hyde Park, New York. He attended college and law school. His cousin Theodore became president of the United States in 1901. From that time, Franklin was interested in government. Franklin married his distant cousin, Eleanor Roosevelt, in 1905. They had five children: Anna, James, Elliot, Franklin, Jr., and John.

"Ours is a land...filled with happy homes; blessed with comfort and opportunity. I have no fears for the future of our country. It is bright with hope." Herbert Hoover spoke these words. He summed up the mood of the country as he became president of the United States on March 4, 1929.

The 1920s had been great years. Most Americans who wanted a job could have one. One out of every five Americans owned a car. Everyone went to the movies, often two or three times a week. Charlie Chaplin and Mae West were the stars of Hollywood. Babe Ruth was slugging home runs in baseball. Charles Lindbergh became the first pilot to fly solo non-stop across the Atlantic Ocean.

▼ Roosevelt was governor of the most populated state. His office was in the state **capital**: Albany, New York. Roosevelt sat in a wheelchair made from a kitchen chair.

F.D.R.

Franklin Delano Roosevelt grew up in Hyde Park, New York. At the age of 29, he was a state **senator**. At 31, President Woodrow Wilson chose him to be assistant **Secretary of the Navy**. Roosevelt enjoyed working in government.

In 1921, Roosevelt's courage was put to a test. At the age of 39, he got a disease called infantile paralysis, or polio. He could not move his legs. They were paralyzed. Doctors told him to exercise to keep the disease from getting worse. F.D.R. built up his strength by swimming for hours at a time. He wore leg braces and used a cane. He often needed a wheelchair. None of this stopped F.D.R. from following his dreams. In 1928, he was elected governor of New York.

Governor Roosevelt

Many New Yorkers were enjoying the good life of the 1920s. However, Roosevelt knew that not all New Yorkers were doing well. He investigated the problems of New York farmers and factory workers. He suggested programs to improve their schools, lower their **taxes**, and provide less expensive electricity.

▲◄ In the 1920s, some Americans earned money by selling goods from pushcarts (above left) or working in factories (above). Others were farmers, like the couple in the photograph opposite. By 1929, many farmers were starving, as their crops failed, and their workers left for better-paying jobs in cities.

▼ This photograph was taken in 1932. It includes Franklin (seated bottom left) and Eleanor, their children, grandchildren, and Franklin's mother, Sara.

▼ Many Americans became rich during the 1920s. Some owned large businesses called corporations. Others ran banks that loaned money to build houses.

PANIC IN THE STOCK MARKET

Americans felt confident about the country's big businesses. Large companies, such as U.S. Steel and American Telephone and Telegraph (AT&T), were making lots of money. Any American could own a part of these rich companies by buying stocks in the companies through the stock market.

Here is how the **stock market** works. Stocks are shares of a business. They are for sale in the stock market. You might buy a share of stock for $10. If the company becomes successful, your share could be worth more money. You could sell that stock or hold it to see if it is worth more tomorrow. In the late 1920s, the prices of many stocks kept getting higher. It seemed easy to make money in the stock market. Millions of Americans bought stocks. Many of them borrowed money from banks to buy more stocks.

In late fall of 1929, stock prices started to drop. A $10 share of stock might have been worth $5. People rushed to sell their stocks before they lost too much money. This made stock prices drop more.

▲ This was the front page of *The New York Times* on October 30, 1929. The stock market panic lasted for many weeks. Some people in business and government hoped that things would improve. But, by the end of 1929, many Americans had lost all their money, their jobs, and their homes.

▶ Hard times fall on many Americans. This man who once had a high-paying job now needs money badly. He may have bought this car last year for $300. Today, he will be lucky to sell it for $50. Few people can afford to buy cars. Most of the automobile companies have stopped producing new cars.

▶ This man is called a trader. He buys and sells stocks. On October 24, 1929, he will gamble by buying stocks during the panic. Stock prices are very low. They may rise soon. But they could drop lower. In fact, on October 29, the stock market crashes. There are no buyers for stocks. Stock owners have gone broke.

Prices tumble, the market "crashes"

On October 29, 1929, every shareholder tried to sell their stocks. Almost no one wanted to buy them. The stocks became worthless. People who had used their life savings to buy stocks now had no money. People who had borrowed money from banks to buy stocks were now in **debt**. Most people could not afford to buy new products. So many companies closed down or at least produced less. They fired their workers. Millions of Americans now had no jobs.

▶ Stock exchanges are places where stocks are bought and sold. The Stock Exchange on Wall Street in New York City is one of the most important. On October 29, 1929, many shareholders called the Stock Exchange, trying to sell their stocks. Outside, crowds gathered awaiting news of the market crash, as in the photo above.

HARD TIMES

America's good times ended quickly. The nation's finances were in trouble. Then, the stock market collapsed in 1929. People lost their savings and then their jobs and their homes. The hard times lasted until 1939. These years are called the Great Depression.

The **stock market** crash signaled the start of the Great **Depression**. America's factories were over-producing. Machines worked at such great speed that goods were produced faster than people could buy them. By 1929, unsold goods were piling up. Companies started to produce less. They let some of their employees go and put others on part-time work. When people lost their income, they bought even less. Companies sold fewer goods. Many had to close down. By 1932, one out of every three Americans was unemployed, or out of work.

▶ When people heard about the bank failures, they ran to get their money. Those who arrived late found the bank doors locked. By winter of 1932–1933, about 5,000 banks closed. Nine million people lost their savings. Today the government **insures** bank accounts so that this will not happen again.

F.D.R. versus Hoover
As New York's governor, Franklin Roosevelt had new ideas to help New Yorkers. He started programs to put people back to work. He created jobs planting trees and improving farm land. Many Americans thought President Herbert Hoover should use these ideas throughout the country. President Hoover disagreed. "People must fight their own battles in their own communities," he said.

10

Banks close too

During the good times of the 1920s, people saved their money at banks. Many banks used most of their customers' savings to buy stocks. The banks lost this money when the stock market crashed. Banks had another problem. Many people had borrowed money from banks. When the Depression started, people could not pay back their loans. As a result, hundreds of banks ran out of money and closed. People could not get back their savings.

◀ Many Americans were too poor to buy food. They stood in **"bread lines"** to get free food. This photo was taken in February 1932 in New York City.

◀ This farmer is giving up on his fields. People can only pay a few cents for a sackful of corn. It is not worth harvesting.

▶ This man once owned a clothing business. Now he worries that he will never earn another dollar. He worries most about his children. There is not enough food for them to eat every day.

◀ Some people lost their homes because they could not pay their **mortgage**. They wandered to a poor section of town and built shacks out of wooden boxes, as here in Seattle, Washington. People called these areas Hoovervilles. They blamed President Hoover for their troubles.

PRESIDENT ROOSEVELT

Millions of Americans were jobless, homeless, and feeling hopeless. Could the country that had grown so strong fall apart now? Americans looked to their government leaders for help. President Hoover believed the government should not get involved. In 1932, Franklin Roosevelt ran for president.

Ban on alcohol ends
In December 1933, **Prohibition** ended with the 21st **Amendment**. Roosevelt was in favor of the amendment. Many Americans argued that Prohibition took away personal freedom. Also, the liquor industry could create jobs and tax money. The 21st Amendment repealed, or cancelled, the 18th Amendment for Prohibition.

▲ This photo was taken in October 1932 in Indianapolis, Indiana. Roosevelt is running for president against the current president, Herbert Hoover. During the 1932 campaign, Roosevelt visited 38 of the 48 states. He traveled 27,000 miles (43,400 kilometers), many of them on a train called "the Roosevelt Special." Roosevelt won the **election** by seven million votes.

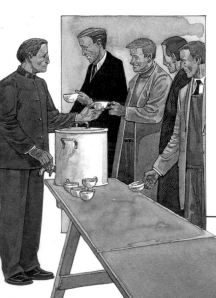

◀ Many people were embarrassed to stand in line for free food. But jobs in the New Deal programs paid only $30 to $50 a month, which was not enough to house and feed a family. Communities set up **soup kitchens** to feed hungry people.

Roosevelt promised Americans a "new deal." He would help create government programs so that people could make money and support themselves again. Roosevelt won the presidential **election** in 1932 and at his **inauguration** he gave America hope by saying, "This great nation will endure.... The only thing we have to fear is fear itself."

President Roosevelt called on **Congress** to get his ideas going quickly. The new programs paid people to develop parks and to build roads, schools, and hydroelectric dams. Farmers received money to run their farms again. Roosevelt wanted people to earn money so they could buy goods. Then the factories could reopen and hire more people.

New Hope
Roosevelt's **New Deal** did not end the **Depression**. But it gave many Americans jobs, homes, and—most of all—new confidence in America's businesses and government. Many New Deal programs continued for more than 65 years and are important parts of America today. They include minimum wage laws and Social Security payments (for Americans who are too old or not able to work).

▲ Farmland in the Tennessee River valley was poor. Scientists developed fertilizers to make the soil better.

Informing the people

President Roosevelt regularly talked to the American people over the radio during "fireside chats." He explained how he planned to improve things. "He said he understood what we were going through," remembers Rachel Hasson, whose parents owned a grocery store in Los Angeles, California. "For many years, his fireside chats made us feel that everything would be OK."

◀ One of the biggest projects of the New Deal took place in the Tennessee River valley. The river often flooded. In 1933, the Tennessee Valley Authority (T.V.A.) hired workers to build 40 **dams** along the river and its branches. The dams stopped flooding and created cheap electric power.

▲ Roosevelt gives a fireside chat.

THE DUST BOWL

The Dust Bowl of the 1930s

Dear Mrs. Roosevelt: "For the first time of my lifetime I am asking a favor. Among your friends do you know of one who is discarding a spring coat? If so could you beg the old one for me? We were hit very hard by the drought and every penny we can save goes [for the crops] ."

This letter was sent on May 10, 1935, from a farm woman from Goff, Kansas, part of America's Dust Bowl. This region got its name during a seven-year drought in the 1930s. A drought means there was very little rain. In the 1920s, farmers had unwisely plowed up acres of grassland to plant wheat. By 1934, there were no grassy roots to hold the soil down. There was no rain to keep it down either. Then the wind storms came.

▼ ▲ This family is fixing its car as they prepare to move out of the Dust Bowl, leaving their land and their home. The father and oldest son hope to get work on farms farther west. In 1935 alone, about 40 big storms had swept across their land.

Clouds of dust

Whenever the wind blew through the Dust Bowl, the soil lifted up off the fields. It blew across the land in a thick dusty cloud. Cattle choked. People suffered from lung damage. Cars' engines and farm machines were ruined.

Moving out

Farmers in the Dust Bowl felt hopeless. Thousands of families decided to leave their farms for good. Some packed up and went to big cities. Many headed to California. They hoped to find jobs on farms and a better life there. However, there were many more new arrivals to California than there were jobs for them.

Help to farmers

The president and **Congress** tried to help farmers through these bad times. They passed laws to give **relief** money to families in the Dust Bowl. They passed the Agricultural Adjustment Act. Farmers in other regions were paid not to grow certain crops. Fewer crops meant farmers could charge higher prices for food.

▲ A Dust Bowl scene. This photo was taken at Dallas, South Dakota, on May 13, 1936. Millions of tons of soil turned to dust and blew all the way to the East Coast. Sailors 20 miles (32 kilometers) off the coast in the Atlantic Ocean said they swept Dust Bowl dust off the decks of their ship.

◄ This poster was created for the U.S. government by Ben Shahn. Many writers and artists created works about the Dust Bowl struggles. John Steinbeck wrote a famous novel called *The Grapes of Wrath*. Songwriter Woody Guthrie (who wrote *This Land Is Your Land*) wrote *Hard Traveling* about the farmers who left the Dust Bowl.

Changes on reservations
For about 100 years, the U.S. government operated Native American **reservations** where Native American religions were banned. In 1934, the government ended this policy and said Native Americans could live according to their traditions. Congress also passed the Indian Reorganization Act. It protected the land on Native American reservations from development.

WORK PROGRAMS

It cost millions of dollars to create new jobs. It would have been cheaper to simply give people money. But Roosevelt said: "Most Americans want to give something for what they get.... Honest work is the saving barrier between them and moral disintegration."

In May 1935, the government set up the Works Progress Administration (W.P.A.). It came up with "small useful projects." Some workers repaired sidewalks and roads. Others built playgrounds.

The W.P.A. gave work to artists, actors, musicians, and writers. Artists painted **murals** and carved statues for public buildings. Actors staged operas and puppet shows. Musicians performed concerts. Writers created guidebooks for every state. About 8,500,000 people got jobs through the W.P.A.

▼ This artist, Alfred Castagne, was paid by the WPA to make a sketch of these workers. The workers were paid by the WPA to build curbs on a street in Michigan.

▼ The government paid artists to paint pictures to brighten up buildings. Some of these paintings hang in the White House and can still be seen in other public buildings.

Helping the disabled

F.D.R. spent as much time as he could in Warm Springs, Georgia. Since 1924, he went there for treatments for his polio. He swam in pools filled with warm natural spring water. In 1926, he started the Warm Springs Foundation. It provided low-cost treatments to other people with polio. Roosevelt called his home at Warm Springs "The Little White House."

▼ This was a recruitment poster for the Civilian Conservation Corps (C.C.C.). Between 1933 and 1942, this organization gave work and training in forestry, farming, flood control, and clearing up to more than 2,500,000 young people. The poster was designed by the Illinois W.P.A. Art Project.

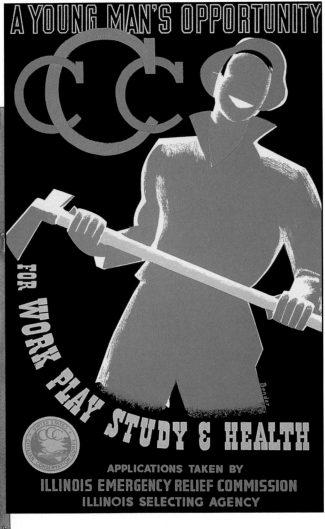

The 1936 election

Roosevelt ran for president again in 1936 and won. In his second **inauguration** speech, he said: "The test of our progress is not whether we add more to the abundance of those who have much; it is whether we provide enough for those who have too little."

Critics

Not everyone loved F.D.R. and his ideas. Many people criticized the **New Deal** programs. The government did not have the money to pay the workers in all the new programs. The government spent more than it had and it was in **debt**. It raised some **taxes** to ease the situation. Other critics said the programs favored workers, but were unfair to big business owners. Still other critics feared that people would get used to government paychecks. They would not want to seek jobs in private businesses again.

▼ Many of today's roads, airports, and parks were built as W.P.A. projects. By 1940, the W.P.A. had constructed or rebuilt 200,000 buildings and bridges and 600,000 miles (965,000 kilometers) of roads and water pipes (below left). Some W.P.A. jobs were as small as sawing wood (below right). Poor people received the wood to burn for heat.

◄ Some W.P.A. workers, like these women, sewed clothing. Others canned vegetables or made books and maps in Braille for blind people. The W.P.A. was run by Frances Perkins, Roosevelt's Secretary of Labor. She was the first woman to hold a senior government job.

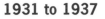

BUILDING THE TALLEST AND LONGEST

Americans have always had grand ideas—wanting to move faster, fly farther, and communicate better. Some of America's grand plans stalled during the Depression. Other plans became reality and set new records, both for America and the world.

During the rich days of the 1920s, a group of builders dreamed up New York City's Empire State Building. By the time construction was completed in 1931, the **Depression** was under way. Businesses were closing. Few people wanted to rent office space in the world's tallest building. Some people jokingly called it the "Empty State Building."

Despite the empty offices, the 102-floor building amazed people. At 1,250 feet (381 meters) high, it seemed like a real "skyscraper." It towered over the rest of New York City. Anyone who could scrape together an extra dollar stood in line to ride the elevator up to the top floors to look down upon the toy-size city below.

Golden Gate Bridge

In 1937, builders in San Francisco, California, built the longest bridge in the world. The 8,931-foot (2,722-meter) bridge spanned the entrance of San Francisco Bay. The bridge has a six-lane road that helps people travel from northern California to the peninsula of San Francisco. Many bridges have been built since 1937. The Golden Gate Bridge is still one of the longest suspension bridges and is a major tourist attraction.

▶ In the 1930s, many people wanted to travel by derigible. On May 6, 1937, the German-built *Hindenburg* exploded while docking in Lakehurst, New Jersey. Thirty-five of the 97 passengers died.

▼ This photograph, by Lewis Hine, was taken while the Empire State Building was under construction. In the 1970s, it was overtaken in height with the construction of the 1,350-foot (412-meter) World Trade Center in New York City and the 1,454-foot (443-meter) Sears Tower in Chicago, Illinois.

◀ Photographers soar by San Francisco's Golden Gate Bridge in a small airplane. They get a bird's-eye view of the construction of the world's longest bridge at that time.

▲ The Grand Coulee **Dam** is the largest concrete dam in the country. It was built from 1934 to 1942 and spans the Columbia River in Washington State.

▼ In 1936, the McDonnell Douglas company began making passenger planes for Trans World Airlines (T.W.A.). Each plane carried 21 passengers. The passenger aircraft could travel across the country in less than 24 hours, but had to stop several times for fuel.

MAKING A LIVING

The Depression changed the lives of many Americans. People who had once been rich took jobs shining shoes and planting trees. They spent money only on necessities: food, shelter, and medicine. Even when times got better, these people saved their money. They had trouble treating themselves to a new pair of shoes or a restaurant meal.

Another election
It was time for another presidential **election** in 1940. F.D.R. already had served two terms. No other president ever tried to serve more. Critics said that it was time for a change. Modifying a quote used by Abraham Lincoln during the 1864 elections, F.D.R. said: "Don't change horses in midstream." Franklin Roosevelt won the election for a third time.

Children knew they were living in tough times. Some went out to work at the age of 13 so they could give money to their families. Most children had to make do with homemade, improvised toys. Scraps of fabrics were made into dolls. A mass of string became a ball. Children got used to wearing extra-big clothing. Parents bought too-big clothes so children would not outgrow them too soon.

Eleanor Roosevelt

Most Americans admired the president's wife, the nation's "first lady," Eleanor Roosevelt. Since she could travel more easily than the president, she traveled the country talking to people and checking on government projects.

Eleanor visited workers in coal mines and spoke to people in unemployment lines. People called her the "eyes and ears of the president." She also wrote a newspaper column and had her own radio program. She was more active than any other first lady before her.

▶ Mrs. Roosevelt spent most of her life helping people. In this photo, taken in New York in 1932, she is serving food at a **soup kitchen**. She also visited hospitals, schools, and factories.

▼ In the 1930s, nine million workers belonged to **unions** so they could fight for better pay and working conditions. These are workers from Ford Motor Company.

▼ People who managed to keep their jobs lived comfortably. Rent in a housing development in Washington, D.C., was $20 to $45 a month. People who had money could buy goods at low "**Depression**" prices. This family has a modern electric stove, which became popular in the 1930s.

◄ Mechanical refrigerators (far left) became popular in the 1920s, but every few years a bigger and better model was introduced. Automatic washing machines (left) were a new household convenience introduced in 1937. They saved hours of washing each piece of clothing by hand.

21

TAKING A BREAK

Americans wanted relief from the worries of the Depression. They often turned to a large wooden box in the living room: the radio. In the 1930s, two out of every three homes had a radio. That was double the number of homes with telephones.

Families gathered around a radio the way families today watch television. Radios brought major league baseball teams, such as the Brooklyn Dodgers and Boston Braves, into millions of homes. Radios also brought world news, as a major war heated up in Europe.

Most of all, radios brought lively entertainment. There were music shows, played by live bands. There were comedy shows with George Burns, Gracie Allen, and Jack Benny. Like many radio stars, these people later became TV stars.

▼ In 1936, a writer named Margaret Mitchell wrote *Gone With the Wind.* This romantic **Civil War** story became the best-selling book in America. In 1939, the story was made into the longest movie of the 1930s (3 hours). It also made the most money.

▼ Americans could not seem to get enough baseball. The first All-Star Game was played in Comiskey Park in Chicago on July 6, 1933. The Baseball Hall of Fame opened in Cooperstown, New York, in 1939. Babe Ruth, Lou Gehrig, Joe DiMaggio, and Dizzy Dean were American heroes.

America's favorites:
1931 the movie *Dracula*
1932 game of Monopoly created by Charles B. Darrow
1933 movie *King Kong*
1933 first comic book: *Funnies on Parade*
1936 book *Uncle Tom's Cabin*, written in the 1850s, is a best-seller
1937 the first full-length animated film, Walt Disney's *Snow White and the Seven Dwarfs*
1937 first *Bugs Bunny* cartoon
1938 first *Superman* action comic book
1940 M&M candies first sold

In new screen splendor...
The most magnificent picture ever!

DAVID O. SELZNICK'S PRODUCTION OF MARGARET MITCHELL'S
"GONE WITH THE WIND"

◀ African American Jesse Owens was the star of the 1936 Olympics in Berlin, Germany. Owens won four gold medals in track and field. This annoyed many Germans, who believed black people were inferior.

Movies

Americans also loved to escape to movie theaters. In 1938, almost 80 million movie tickets were sold each week. For a quarter, you could watch a movie, a cartoon, a **newsreel**, and eat two boxes of candy. In 1939, *The Wizard of Oz* was one of America's favorite movies. It tells of a girl's escape from a Kansas farm during the **Depression**. She arrives in the colorful land of Oz and later realizes "there's no place like home." Like most movies then, there was a happy ending.

Americans also enjoyed watching happy stories with child stars Shirley Temple and Mickey Rooney. There was also the comedy of the Marx Brothers and the suspense created by Alfred Hitchcock.

◀ The radio was an important piece of furniture. It was the focal point of every home. Everyone had a favorite show. Children ran home from school to listen to radio adventure stories. Millions of women tuned into dramatic stories filled with joy and tears. Soap companies advertised during these programs, giving them the name "soap operas." Programs lasted between 15 and 60 minutes.

World War II Begins in Europe

When World War I ended in 1918, it was called the "war to end all wars." But peace did not last. German people were angry. Germany had lost land in that war. Germany's government owed money to other countries for war damages. By 1930, German people had more problems because the Depression hit Germany too.

Thousands of Germans were jobless and homeless. They wanted a strong leader to end their troubles. A former soldier named Adolf Hitler made public speeches, saying he could make Germany great again. Hitler became Germany's leader in 1933. He turned out to be a very dangerous leader. He made himself a **dictator** and took total control of the government. He blamed such groups as Jews, immigrants, and disabled people for Germany's problems. Soon he had these people arrested and sent to prisons called **concentration camps**.

F.D.R. plans for war
The president felt America would need to help Britain and France stop Hitler. On January 6, 1941, he spoke to Americans: "No nation could remain either safe or free unless protected by a united world order founded on 'four essential freedoms': freedom of speech, freedom of worship, freedom from want, and freedom from fear."
F.D.R. asked **Congress** for money to buy **military** weapons and supplies.

▲ German U-boats (submarines) tried to destroy American supply ships before they reached Europe. This is the view of a supply ship through the lens of the U-boat periscope. In September of 1940, U-boats sank 27 **Allied** ships in the Atlantic.

▲ Adolf Hitler ruled Germany as a dictator from 1933 to 1945. He ordered millions of people killed because he felt they threatened his power.

▲ Benito Mussolini ruled Italy for 21 years, most of them as a dictator. In 1940, he sent his soldiers to join Hitler's soldiers in taking over France.

▼ Italy, Germany, and Japan were called the Axis Powers. Britain and France, later joined by the Soviet Union and the United States, were called the Allies. This map shows Europe in 1943, before Italy surrendered to the Allies.

World War II in Europe by 1943

Allied areas	☐
Axis countries	☐
Axis occupied areas	☐
Neutral countries	☐

Norway, Sweden, Finland, Denmark, United Kingdom, Eire, Netherlands, Belgium, Germany, Normandy, Brittany, Switzerland, France, Portugal, Spain, Italy, Sicily, Estonia, Latvia, Lithuania, Poland, Czechoslovakia, Austria, Hungary, Romania, Yugoslavia, Bulgaria, Albania, Greece, Soviet Union, Turkey, Syria, Lebanon, Iraq, Palestine, Saudi Arabia, Morocco, Algeria, Tunisia, Libya, Egypt

The road to war

Hitler and his party, called **Nazis**, took control of Germany. They outlawed freedom of the press. They banned people from moving, changing jobs, or traveling without permission. They began training young Germans aged 6 to 18 to be loyal German soldiers. They taught children to spy on their families and to report parents who spoke against the Nazis.

Then Hitler set out to control the world. In 1938 and 1939, he took over Austria and Czechoslovakia. In September 1939, he took over Poland. France and Britain wanted to help Poland. They declared war on Germany. World War II began.

▲ This photo was taken in Warsaw in Poland in 1940. Starting in 1939, all Jews in Germany and Poland had to wear a yellow Star of David sewn onto their clothes so the police could watch their movements.

▶ By 1941, Britain had run out of money and ships. She was fighting alone—a small island against a Europe now occupied by Germany. America began sending airplanes, ships, and weapons to Britain. The ships in the background are called Liberty ships. They were made in the United States and sailed to Europe across the Atlantic Ocean. The ship in front is an American destroyer.

UNITED STATES AT WAR

Winston Churchill, Britain's prime minister, was listening to the 9 P.M. radio news on December 7, 1941. With great surprise, he ran to call President Roosevelt. "What's this about Japan?" Churchill asked. "It's quite true," said F.D.R. "They have attacked us at Pearl Harbor. We are all in the same boat now."

In the 1930s and 1940s, Japan attacked and took over parts of China and southeast Asia (later called Vietnam, Cambodia, and Laos). As punishment, the United States and Britain stopped selling oil and other goods to Japan. Japan's leaders, Emperor Hirohito and Hideki Tojo, resented this interference. Tojo decided to stop the United States with **military** force. His air force bombed the American naval base in Pearl Harbor, Hawaii. Nineteen U.S. ships and 150 planes were destroyed and about 2,400 people were killed.

▼ The Pearl Harbor attack made Americans fearful of the Japanese Americans who lived in the U.S. In March 1942, F.D.R. ordered more than 110,000 Japanese Americans living on the West Coast to sell their homes and move to special camps.

▲ Hideki Tojo was a military leader. In 1941, he became Japan's premier (government leader). On December 6, 1941, F.D.R. wrote to Tojo asking that "our two great countries... restore traditional [friendship] and prevent further destruction in the world." The next day Tojo ordered the attack on Pearl Harbor.

F.D.R. speaks
On December 8, F.D.R. spoke to an emergency session of **Congress**. "Yesterday, December 7, 1941...the United States of America was attacked by naval and air forces of the Empire of Japan. Always will we remember the character of the attack against us. ...[We will] make very certain that this form of treachery shall never endanger us again. With confidence in our armed forces—with the unbounded determination of our people—we will gain the inevitable triumph—so help us God." Then the president asked Congress to declare war on Japan. In just 33 minutes, it was done.

Joining the war

F.D.R. heard about the Pearl Harbor attack in a call from the **Secretary of the Navy**. F.D.R.'s advisors ran to the White House. The President immediately prepared a message to the nation. The next day, the U.S. Congress declared war on Japan. Britain and Canada did the same. Three days later, Japan's friends—Germany and Italy—declared war on the United States. For the second time in 25 years, America was at war. Americans were ready to help. Thousands rushed to sign up for military service. Factories that had been closed during the **Depression** opened their doors again. They began making tanks, guns, planes, and ammunition. Factories needed workers again. The Depression was over!

The early war years
1939
Sept. 1 Germany invades Poland
Sept. 3 Britain and France declare war on Germany; World War II begins
1940
April Germany takes over Denmark and Norway
May Germany takes over Holland and Belgium
June German army marches into Paris. France surrenders
July–October Germany bombs Britain, but the R.A.F. defeats its air force; Japan joins **Axis Powers**
1941
June Germany invades the Soviet Union; Soviet Union joins the Allied Powers;
Dec. Japan bombs Pearl Harbor, Hawaii; U.S. enters the war

◀ On Sunday morning, December 7, U.S. battleships were lined up in Pearl Harbor, Hawaii. At 7:55 A.M., Japanese planes flew overhead and dropped bombs. This picture shows sailors trying to rescue the crew of the battleship *West Virginia*.

THE U·S·MARINES WANT YOU ENLIST TODAY

◀ This 1942 poster encouraged Americans to join the **Marines**. Five million Americans volunteered for military service. Ten million were drafted. That means the government required them to serve.

27

REPORTING FOR DUTY

When the United States joined the war, the Allied countries cheered. They knew that America was the world's richest nation. It had plenty of factories, people, and resources such as steel. America's navy would become the largest in the world.

▼ President Roosevelt (right) met with Britain's **Prime Minister** Winston Churchill in August 1941. They planned their goals for fighting the **Axis Powers**. They signed the **Atlantic Charter**.

In 1943, over 2,500,000 men and women joined the U.S. **military** service. Most left for Britain, Italy, northern Africa, and the Pacific islands on ocean liners. Life as a soldier took great courage. No matter how often they faced the enemy's guns, the soldiers never got used to combat. They fought through hunger, cold, and fear for many reasons. They loved their country. They hated the enemies of freedom. Most of all, they felt responsible for their fellow soldiers and would not let them down.

► More than 15 million men and 300,000 women served in the U.S. military during WWII.
1. About 2,411,000 served in the Army Air Force.
2. About a million African Americans served in WWII. Rarely were they **segregated** from white members. Many of them worked as mechanics.
3. Soldiers were often called G.I.s because their equipment was stamped G.I. meaning "Government Issue."
4. Over 3,400,000 men and women served as sailors on U.S. ships.
5. Over 40,000 women served on air bases.

1. Pilot

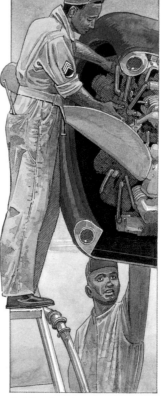

2. Mechanic

3. G.I.

Fighting around the world

Americans joined **Allied** troops in North Africa and Europe, and on islands in the Pacific. In Europe, the Germans seemed unbeatable. They had taken over most of the continent. Their submarines sank ships faster than the Allies could replace them. In North Africa, U.S. and British troops led by General Dwight Eisenhower took over Morocco and Algeria. They trapped German troops led by General Erwin Rommel in Tunisia. By May 1943, the Allies had won in North Africa.

In the Pacific, Americans faced Japanese troops on islands such as Guadalcanal, Guam, Iwo Jima, and New Guinea. Allied forces won important Pacific victories, particularly in the Battle of Midway, when American planes sank four Japanese aircraft carriers.

▼ On Pacific islands, American troops faced not only stifling heat, poisonous insects, and deadly diseases, but also skilled Japanese soldiers who would rather die fighting than **surrender**.

4. Sailor   5. Air Force Women

▲ American factories stopped making automobiles and radios and began making tanks and planes. This equipment helped the Allies win World War II (often shortened to WWII or called the Second World War). This is a photo of an American-made Stuart tank rolling through North Africa in 1942.

THE HOME FRONT

America needed all its citizens to help win the war. While millions of men left home to fight, millions of women stepped into their jobs. Some assembled planes. Others took over neighborhood jobs, such as driving buses and pumping gas.

The war affected every American family. Farmers grew more food than ever. The government bought it and sent it to its soldiers and sailors. That made food scarce for everyone at home. The government set a limit on how much sugar, butter, coffee, and meat each family could buy every month. Millions of Americans planted "victory gardens" in their backyards and even on city rooftops. These gardens fed their families while the government sent food overseas.

Shortages and reusing metals

There were other shortages on the home front. Tire factories stopped making car tires so they could make tires for buses and trucks. People had to patch and repatch their old tires. The **military** also needed gasoline. Citizens could only get limited amounts of gas for their cars.

Shoe factories stopped making shoes and made military boots instead. Dress factories made U.S. Army, Navy, and Air Force uniforms. Few people bought new clothes during the war. A trade developed in secondhand goods. The government asked Americans to collect scrap metal for the weapons factories. Citizens turned over toothpaste tubes, old lawn mowers, bicycles, and license plates.

▼ The government gave every family ration books, or food allowance, stamps like these. At the food store, you could use a stamp to buy a pound (450 grams) of sugar every two weeks.

War and the White House

Before war broke out, Franklin and Eleanor Roosevelt entertained frequently at the White House. They had 13 grandchildren, who often stayed with them. An indoor swimming pool was installed in the White House so that F.D.R. could exercise. After the U.S. entered the war, the Roosevelts did little entertaining. They both frequently traveled. Their four sons went to war. Worried about enemy attacks on the White House and the president, workers installed machine guns on the White House roof. They built a **bomb shelter** in the basement.

RATION BOOK HOLDER

WAR RATION BOOK FOUR

► This poster encouraged women to help their country by going to work.

▼ America's factories ran day and night. Americans made 300,000 military planes at a cost of $45 billion.

We Can Do It!

What things cost in 1943
- loaf of bread: 9 cents
- gallon of gasoline: 15 cents
- *Time* magazine: 10 cents
- toothpaste: 37 cents
- bottle of soda: 5 cents
- postcard: 1 cent
- airmail stamp: 8 cents
- room for one night at a New York City hotel (with bathroom and radio): $2.50

▲ To keep factories running, five million women took jobs. Advertising posters with pictures of a character called Rosie the Riveter encouraged women to go to work. Thousands of "Rosies" attached airplane parts with fasteners called rivets.

▲ The government paid women and men the same for the same work. However, many employers found ways to pay women less. After the war, many women quit their jobs to become housewives. Others were fired to make jobs available for returning soldiers.

31

ATTACK ON EUROPE

While Americans listened to war news on the radio, Europeans listened to bombs and gunfire outside their homes. In June 1940, Germany conquered France. That August, they began bombing England's major cities. In June 1941, Hitler attacked the Soviet Union. That may have been his costliest mistake.

For 18 months, the Germans successfully stormed through the **Soviet Union**. But the Soviet army gathered its strength and finally ended the **invasion** at Stalingrad. In the winter of 1943, they cut off the German supply lines. German soldiers were freezing and starving to death. That February, the Germans finally left the Soviet Union. Hitler's army never again won another major battle.

On to North Africa and Italy

By May 1943, the **Allies** forced the last **Axis** soldiers out of North Africa. On July 10, 1943, the Allies invaded Sicily, an Italian island between North Africa and mainland Italy. They arrived by air and sea. From there they invaded the Italian mainland. The Italian people were sick of the war. They overthrew their leader Mussolini and put their king back in power. The new government surrendered to the Allies on September 3, 1943, but the war in Italy carried on.

▶ American troops enter the city of Palermo in Sicily. On September 3, 1943, the U.S. Army crossed from Sicily to Italy's mainland. The Italian government surrendered and soon declared war on Germany. German soldiers still occupied much of Italy. Allied soldiers fought their way north to the **capital**, Rome, and took control of it in June 1944.

> **Roosevelt battles on**
> By 1944, Franklin Roosevelt is tired and ill. Still, he campaigns for a fourth term and wins. His war efforts are popular with Americans. No other president has served this long and never will again. Passed in 1951, the 22nd **Amendment** limits any president to two consecutive terms.

▼ U.S. bomber planes try to destroy Germany's weapons factories and railroads. This will not be easy. German radar can spot these planes and anti-aircraft guns try to shoot them out of the sky.

▶ Fighting on the Pacific islands continued. This photo shows United States **Marines** storming ashore at Tarawa in the Gilbert Islands on November 20, 1943.

Bombing Germany

The Allies moved east toward Germany. Tanks and trucks drove overland. Planes buzzed through the skies over German cities. American planes dropped bombs all day. The British dropped bombs at night. At first, Germans shot down many of the bombers and quickly repaired their factories. Eventually the bombs were too much for Germany. The Allies had destroyed most of the weapons factories. Millions of Germans lost their homes or their lives in the bombings.

▲ General George Patton, Jr. led American troops in the invasion of North Africa and the capture of Sicily.

▲ General Douglas MacArthur led the U.S. Army in the South Pacific. His troops freed the Philippine Islands.

VICTORY IN EUROPE

The Allies had a plan. Troops would cross the English Channel from England to Normandy, France. From there, they would move into France and get rid of the enemy. The invasion began June 6, 1944—D-Day. Andy Rooney was there and wrote this passage (printed at the top of the opposite page) in his book, *My War*:

▼ Photographer Robert F. Sargent took this picture in Normandy, France, on D-Day.

◄ On D-Day, 2,700 ships crossed the English Channel, filled with tanks, guns, and soldiers mainly from America, Britain, and Canada. The Germans did not expect them to land in Normandy.

34

"No one can tell the story of D-Day because no one knows it. Each of the 60,000 men who waded ashore that day knew a little part of the story too well. Each knew a friend shot through the throat, shot through the knee....In **Allied** Headquarters in England, the war directors were exultant [happy]. They saw no blood, no dead, no dying. From the **statistician's** point of view the **invasion** was a great success."

Moving in

At first, the Normandy invasion went well for the Allies. But one U.S. attack was a disaster. The Germans were firing guns from all directions. Landing craft brought soldiers and tanks close to the beach, only to hit explosive mines buried in the sea. Whole crews drowned as tanks dropped into the water. Luckily, by nightfall, the surviving Allies managed to get ashore and move into France.

By August 1944, the Allies pushed the Germans out of most of northwestern France. On August 25, the Allies marched into Paris, the French **capital**, and took over the city. France was free!

◀ In August 1944, Allied troops captured St. Malo, Brittany, in northwestern France. This photo shows a U.S. anti-tank gun.

End of the war in Europe
Sept. 3, 1943 Italy surrenders
June 6, 1944 D-Day invasion of Normandy
Aug. 25, 1944 France is liberated, or set free
May 7, 1945 Germany surrenders
May 8, 1945 Victory in Europe (V.E.) Day

Germany's defeat

American, British, and Canadian soldiers pushed through France into Germany. Meanwhile, **Soviet Union** troops pushed the German soldiers out of Poland and moved into Germany. Hitler knew he was defeated. Because he wanted to be the world's most powerful leader but had failed, he killed himself on April 30, 1945. On May 7, Germany **surrendered**.

◀ This cover of a U.S. Army magazine shows a Parisian woman helping American soldiers to speak French. The soldiers have just **liberated** Paris.

SHUTTLE-BOMBING BETWEEN THE U.K. AND RUSSIA

THE HOLOCAUST

Franklin Roosevelt dies
F.D.R. died on April 12, 1945 in Warm Springs, Georgia. As his body was taken to the Washington-bound train, his Warm Springs friends lined up their wheelchairs and waved goodbye. After his funeral in Washington, he was buried at his home in Hyde Park, New York. Vice President Harry S. Truman became president.

As Allied soldiers moved into Europe, they saw the horror of Hitler's power. Hitler had ordered his troops to take millions of people to death camps. The Allied soldiers found these camps filled with starving survivors and millions of dead bodies. The destruction of Jews in particular is called the Holocaust.

In the early 1900s, Jews played a major role in European countries. They were doctors, lawyers, bankers, store owners, writers, and musicians. Hitler, however, thought Jews were evil. He believed his people—white northern Europeans— were superior. As soon as Hitler became Germany's leader, he ordered his soldiers to round up Jews in Holland, France, Austria, Italy, and other countries. Railroad cars filled with Jews headed for the **concentration camps**.

▼ American soldiers **liberate** survivors at a concentration camp in 1945. All the survivors are weak and starving, but thankful. In the camps, strong people were made to work like slaves. The weak were killed in **gas chambers**. The German soldiers had nowhere to bury all the dead so the bodies were burned.

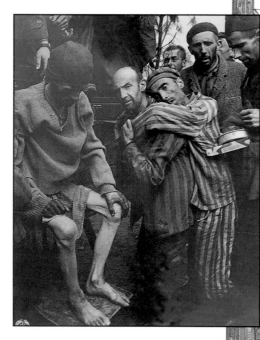

▲ This photo shows Jews in Wobbelin concentration camp in Poland.

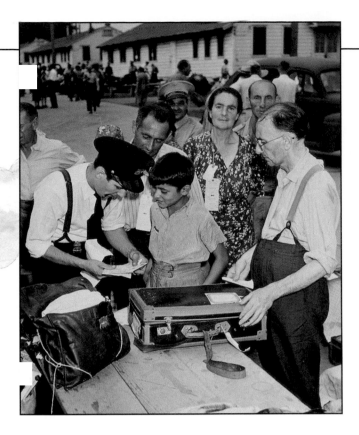

▲ During the 1930s and 1940s, Jews tried to escape Germany and go to the U.S. and friendly European nations such as Britain. However, U.S. **immigration** laws denied them entry. In June 1944, a U.S. government agency managed to get 874 Jews into the country by calling them "prisoners of war." The photo shows some of these people at an army base in Oswego, New York. They were kept there until the the war ended in August 1945.

What happened to the survivors?

Two out of every three European Jews died in concentration camps. That is about six million Jews. Hitler's soldiers also tortured and killed millions of Poles, Slavs, and Gypsies. The **Allied** countries decided to put **Nazi** leaders on trial. In 1945 and 1946, the Nuremberg Trials sentenced 12 Nazi leaders to death. Many other Nazis went to prison.

About 300,000 Jews survived the concentration camps and tried to start their lives again. Many went to their bombed-out communities to search for parents, sisters, brothers, friends. But most Jews were afraid to stay in Europe. About two-thirds (198,000) left for Palestine. It was called the "Jewish homeland" and is now known as Israel. Nearly 72,000 Jews went to the United States; 16,000 to Canada; and 1,000 to Great Britain.

THE WAR ENDS

On the day he died, Roosevelt was writing a speech. It said, "The work, my friends, is peace. More than an end of this war—an end to the beginnings of all wars. Yes, an end, forever, to this impractical, unrealistic settlement of the differences between governments by the mass killing of peoples."

F.D.R. did not live to give that speech, but peace arrived just four months after he wrote it. Peace came with a terrible price. Hundreds of thousands of Japanese people died for it.

The war was not over with the victory in Europe in May 1945. The Japanese would not give up. Americans battled the Japanese to take back islands in the Pacific. American bombs destroyed most of the Japanese navy and air force. Some **Allied** leaders wanted to **invade** Japan. That decision would risk the lives of millions of Allied soldiers. President Truman had another option—an entirely new weapon.

▼ Japan had taken over many islands in the Pacific, including the Philippines, which were once controlled by the U.S. In February 1945, Americans led by General MacArthur took back the Philippines. The United States then introduced a plan called island hopping. This would involve capturing other Japanese-held islands so U.S. forces could get close enough to Japan to launch an invasion. This map shows where major battles took place.

◄ America was succeeding in taking back the Philippines, Iwo Jima, Okinawa, and other Pacific islands. Still, the Japanese fought back. In *kamikaze* attacks, Japanese pilots loaded old planes with bombs and purposely crashed their planes into Allied ships.

World War II in Asia, 1942-1945

U.S.S.R.

ALASKA

Bering Sea

ALEUTIAN ISLANDS

MONGOLIA   MANCHURIA

PACIFIC
OCEAN

Beijing   KOREA   JAPAN
CHINA   Tokyo
         Shanghai   Nagasaki Hiroshima
TIBET   Okinawa   Iwo Jima   Midway Island
INDIA
BURMA   TAIWAN   HAWAIIAN
        Hong   ISLANDS
THAILAND Kong   Pearl
        South Manila   MARIANA   Harbor
        China PHILIPPINES ISLANDS Enewetak
INDOCHINA Sea   Philippine Saipan   MARSHALL
              Leyte Sea   Guam   ISLANDS
              Gulf Peleliu   Kwajalein
MALAYA BRUNEI   Allied areas
Singapore BORNEO   Tarawa GILBERT Japan and Korea
SUMATRA   ISLANDS Areas held by Japan
              NEW   in August 1945
         NETHERLANDS GUINEA Bougainville Neutral countries
         INDIES   SOLOMON
              JAVA   PAPUA   ISLANDS   Major battle
Indian   Guadalcanal   Atomic bombing
Ocean   Darwin   Coral Sea
         AUSTRALIA

N
W   E
S

▼ As the atom bomb exploded on Nagasaki, an enormous fireball filled the sky, followed by a shock wave and heavy winds. This photo shows buildings flattened by the bomb. The bomb's radiation lasted several years and killed 100,000 more people.

Truman's decision

The new weapon was the atomic bomb. It was a powerful weapon that would kill many people and release a long-lasting poison, called **radiation**. Truman spoke to scientists and government leaders to try to make a wise decision. If he dropped the bomb on Japan, thousands of Japanese people would die, including women and children. If the war carried on, thousands of Allied soldiers would die.

On August 6, 1945, an American airplane dropped an atomic bomb on the city of Hiroshima. Over 60,000 people died instantly. At least 40,000 more died in the following days. On August 9, the U.S. dropped a second bomb on the city of Nagasaki, killing 40,000 people and injuring 40,000 more. Japan could take no more. On August 14, 1945, Japan **surrendered**. World War II was over.

◀ In New York City, millions of Americans joined a celebration parade on V-J Day (Victory over Japan Day) on September 2, 1945. On that day, Japanese officials signed the surrender papers.

▼ The photo above shows American and Japanese officials at the surrender ceremony. It was held aboard the battleship USS *Missouri* in Tokyo Bay. Americans throughout the country listened on the radio.

A CHANGING AMERICA

World War II was over. Soldiers, sailors, and pilots returned home. They took back their jobs and married their sweethearts. There were broken hearts for those who did not return. There were still hard times for those who had always been poor. But for millions of Americans, the good times were back.

After the war, millions of couples started families. Between 1946 and 1960, more than 63 million babies were born in the U.S.—more than double the number in the previous 15 years. Those babies would need homes, schools, clothes, food, and entertainment. For years to come, manufacturers would be making products for this group of children. This big jump in the number of births became known as the "baby boom."

Many young families wanted houses with yards or gardens and with garages. They no longer needed to live near their offices or factories in the city. They could buy cars and drive to their workplaces from houses outside the city. Hundreds of neighborhoods sprang up in the **suburbs**. Builders bought farmland and built homes, schools, roads, and stores.

▼ After the war, railroad companies spent billions to get their war-exhausted trains in shape. But business never picked up. Americans were getting used to traveling by cars and planes. This painting by Alexander Leydenfrost shows a 1945 locomotive, *Power*.

▲ No longer did customers stand at a counter and ask for the foods they needed. Now Americans had supermarkets. People walked down aisles and took packages from shelves or out of deep freezers.

▶ Car factories switched from making tanks to making cars again. In 1949, they produced more cars than ever. It seemed like everyone was ready for a new car—especially returning soldiers and families who moved to the suburbs.

Working for equality

African Americans could not live in white neighborhoods or go to white schools. Even America's favorite pastime—baseball—made African Americans play in **Negro** leagues instead of the major leagues. Then, in 1947, African American Jackie Robinson played his first major league game for the Brooklyn Dodgers. Fans and other players shouted bad names at him. He was brave. By the end of that season, he was a star. From that time, baseball has been a game with no color barrier.

▶ A 1947 ad for a refrigerator.

▲ This is an upper middle-class house in the suburbs in 1948. People who lived in a house outside the city needed cars and lawnmowers. Most dads traveled quite a distance to their jobs. Most moms did not work outside the home.

◀ Clothes in 1948 were simple. Women and young girls wore skirts and dresses. They rarely wore pants. Children wore leather shoes every day. They brought sneakers to school for gym class.

41

Historical Map of America

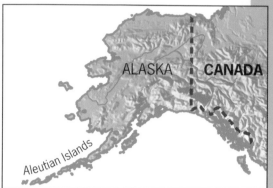

ALASKA CANADA

Aleutian Islands

On the map

By 1948, the United States included 48 states, the territories of Alaska and Hawaii, and the commonwealth of Puerto Rico. All parts of the United States suffered from the Great Depression of the 1930s and 1940s. The farms in the Dust Bowl were already suffering from the country's economic problems. However, America came out of World War II as one of the world's strongest countries. Most Americans once again had jobs and enough money to improve their lives. Millions moved out of cities into sprawling **suburbs**. Opportunities came last to minorities, especially African Americans.

Kauai

Oahu

Maui

Hawaii

HAWAIIAN ISLANDS

PACIFIC OCEAN

Grand Coulee Dam

Seattle

MOUNT RAINIER NATIONAL PARK

Columbia

Spokane

GLACIER NATIONAL PARK

Missouri

WASHINGTON

MONTANA

Portland

OREGON

CRATER LAKE NATIONAL PARK

IDAHO

Snake

Yellowstone

YELLOWSTONE NATIONAL PARK

WYOMING

NEVADA

Salt Lake City

Golden Gate Bridge

San Francisco

YOSEMITE NATIONAL PARK

SEQUOIA NATIONAL PARK

UTAH

COLORADO

Colorado

MESA VERDE NATIONAL PARK

CALIFORNIA

Hollywood Los Angeles

Colorado

ARIZONA

NEW MEXICO

Santa Fé

Rio Grande

ROCKY MOUNTAINS

— River

— Railroad

National parks

······ Highway US1

Dust Bowl areas

Other areas damaged by dust storms

Tennessee Valley Authority dam

| 0 | 250 | 500 miles |
| 0 | 400 | 800 kilometers |

HISTORICAL FICTION TO READ

Crofford, Emily. *A Place to Belong*. Minneapolis: Carolrhoda, 1994. Sixth-grader Tamaladge McLinn and his family are forced to work on an Arkansas cotton plantation after losing their Tennessee farm during the Depression.

Hahn, Mary Downing. *Stepping on the Cracks*. New York:Clarion, 1991. This novel relates a young girl's feelings about World War II.

Lord, Bettie Bao. *In the Year of the Boar and Jackie Robinson*. New York: Harper, 1984. The story of Chinese immigrants in Brooklyn in the late 1940s.

Taylor, Mildred. *Roll of Thunder, Hear My Cry*. New York: Dial, 1976. The story of the Logan family's determination to rise above the prejudice that exists in Mississippi during the 1930s.

HISTORIC SITES TO VISIT

USS *Arizona* Memorial
1 Arizona Memorial Place, Honolulu, Hawaii 96818
Telephone: (808) 541-2693
This memorial to those who died at Pearl Harbor sits in the Pacific Ocean above the sunken USS *Arizona*.

United States Holocaust Memorial Museum
100 Raoul Wallenberg Place SW,
Washington, D.C. 20024. Telephone: (202) 488-0400
This museum presents the story of the six million Jews and millions of others who suffered and died at the hands of the Nazis during World War II.

New York Stock Exchange
20 Broad Street New York, New York 10005
Telephone: (212) 656-5162
You can learn about the history of the stock exchange by viewing exhibits. You can also stand in the visitor's gallery and watch today's trading action.

Home of Franklin D. Roosevelt National Historic Site
519 Albany Post Road, Hyde Park, New York 12538
Telephone: (914) 229-9115
F.D.R. was born in this house and lived here throughout his life. His books, papers, and desk from the White House are on display.

Little White House State Historic Site
401 Little White House Road, Warm Springs, Georgia 31830. Telephone: (706) 655-5870
This is the house where F.D.R. spent his vacations and where he died. Displays depict his life and his role in American history.

Manzanar National Historic Site
P.O. Box 426, Independence, California 93526
Telephone: (619) 878-2932
Japanese Americans were sent here during World War II. Today the grounds and museum tell the story of this chapter in history.

INDEX

Index